Math Games for First Graders

1st Grade Learning Games Series

Speedy Publishing LLC
40 E. Main St. #1156
Newark, DE 19711
www.speedypublishing.com

Color by Number

1
4
9
15

4
4
1
11-2
18-17
9
9
9
9
9
9+6

1
12
14

14-2
8+6
1
9+3
9+5

1
4
5
9
11
15
16
19

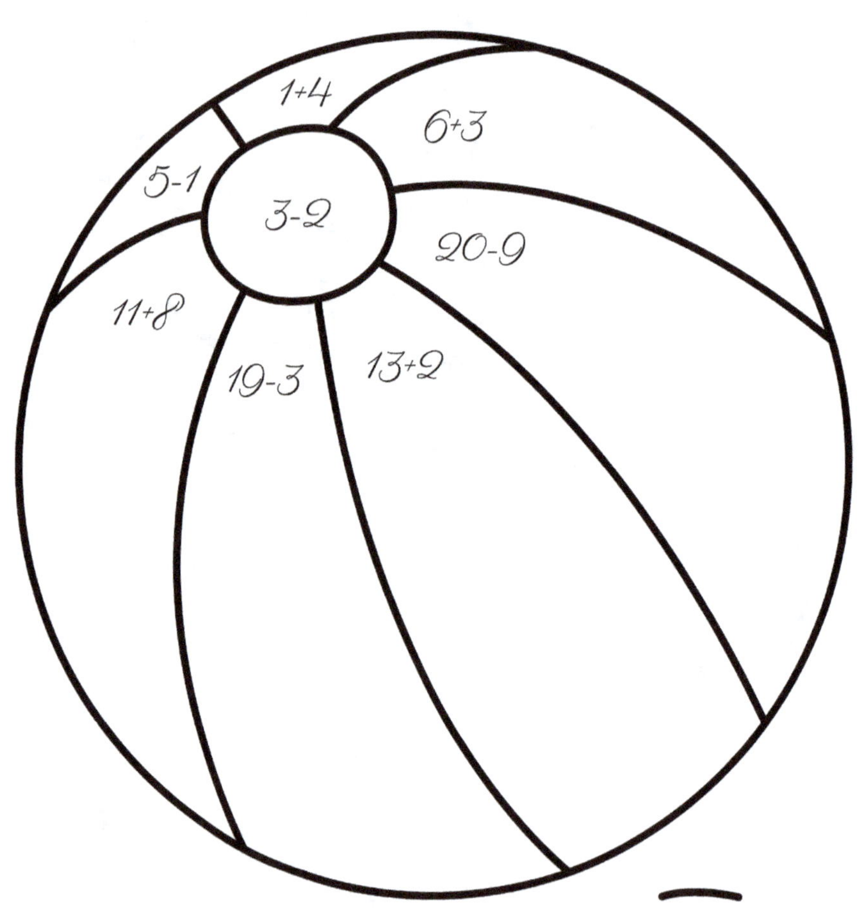
1+4
6+3
5-1
3-2
20-9
11+8
19-3
13+2

8
10
15

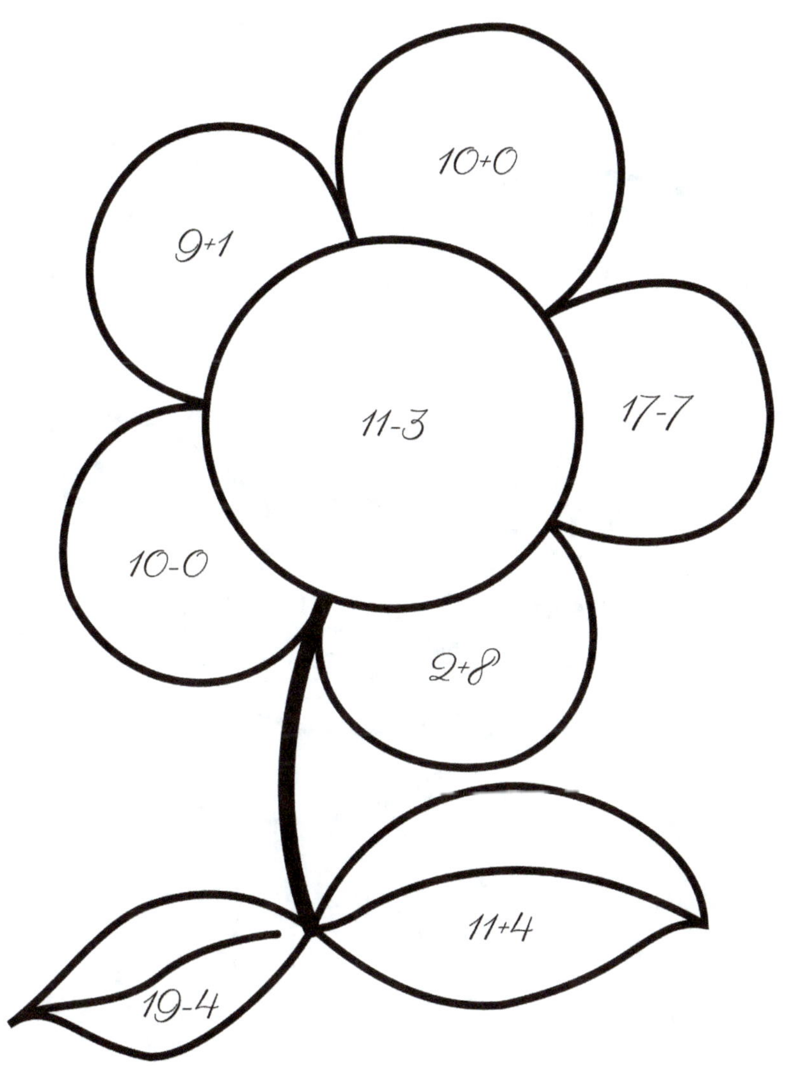
10+0
9+1
11-3
17-7
10-0
2+8
11+4
19-4

1
3
16
19

2-1
11+5
4-3
19
0+1
6-3
8+8

2
10
12

5-3
5+5
5+7

8
9
10

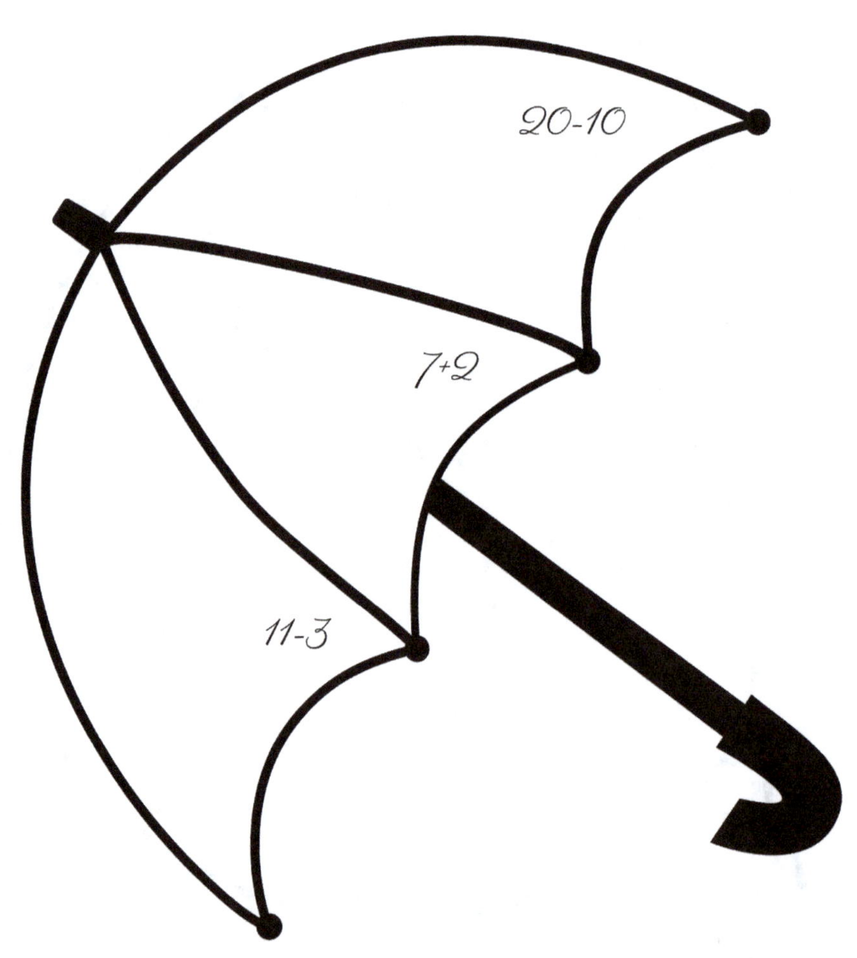
20-10
7+2
11-3

1
5
10
15
20

10
20-15
9+1
7-2
11-1
18+2
1
1
1+0
7+8

1
5
11
19

6+5
20-19
4+1
10+9
1
8+3
1
8+11

1
2
12
17
19

18+1
1+1
2
2
1
11+8
1
20-1
15-3
9+8
10+9

Connect the Dots

Connect the dots from number 1 until you have connected all of them. Then color the picture!

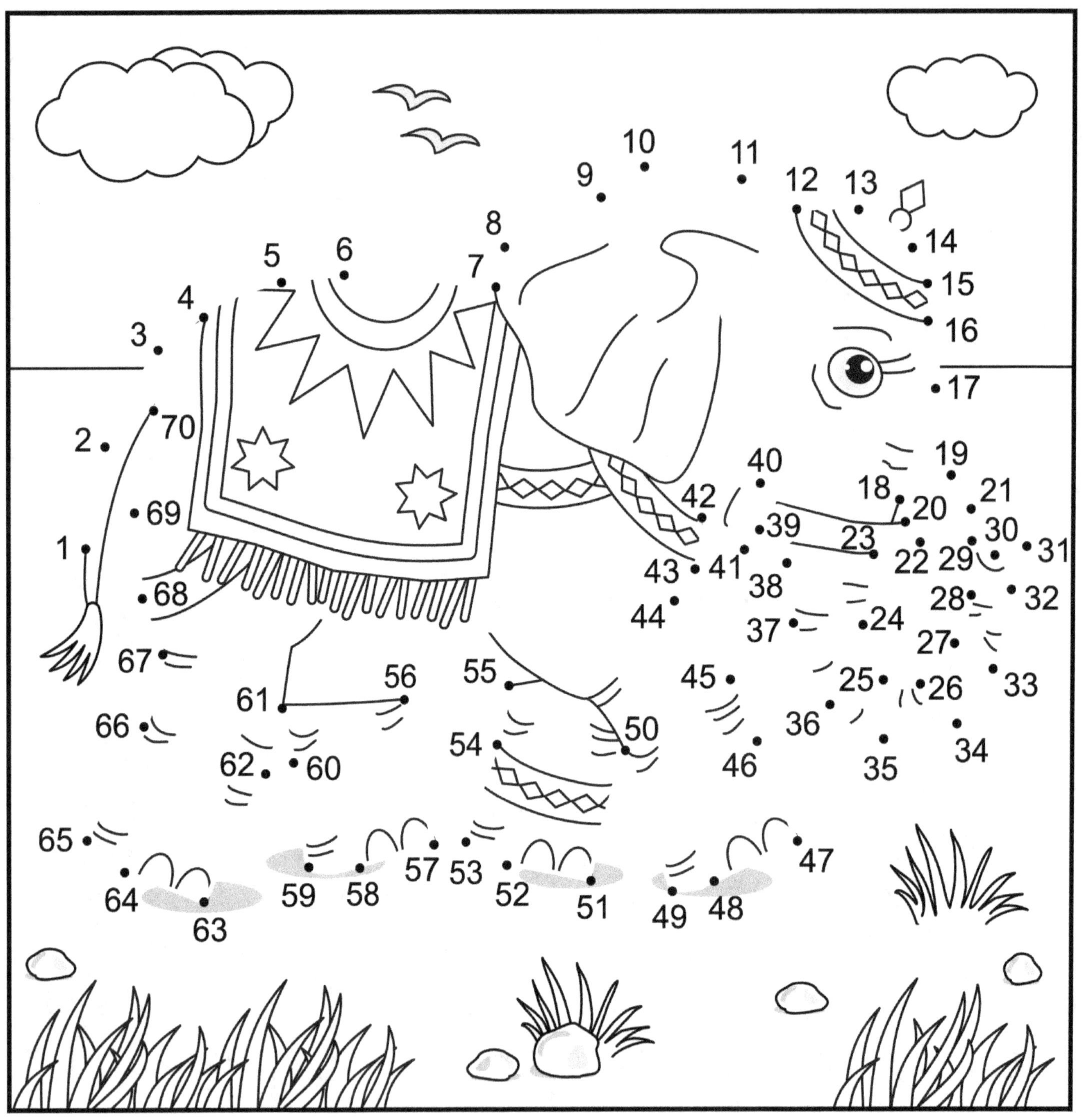

1
2
3
4
5
6
7
8
9
10
11
12
13
14
15
16
17
18
19
20
21
22
23
24
25
26
27
28
29
30
15
20

1
2
3
4
5
6
7
8
9
10
11
12
13
14
15
16
17
18
19
20
21
22
23
24
25

Test your Counting Skills

HOW MANY MONKEYS DO YOU SEE?

HOW MANY FISH DO YOU SEE?

HOW MANY MICE DO YOU SEE?

HOW MANY PIGS DO YOU SEE?

ANSWERS

ANSWERS

ANSWERS

ANSWERS

14 Monkeys

11 Fish

15 Mice

13 Pigs

www.ingramcontent.com/pod-product-compliance
Lightning Source LLC
LaVergne TN
LVHW060833170826
845678LV00010B/1973